A Beautiful Mess

Full Color Version

Kierra Jackson

ROYSTON Publishing

BK Royston Publishing
P. O. Box 4321
Jeffersonville, IN 47131 | 502-802-5385
http://www.bkroystonpublishing.com
bkroystonpublishing@gmail.com

© Copyright – 2020

All Rights Reserved. No part of this book may be reproduced, stored in a retrieval system, or transmitted by any means without the written permission of the author.

Illustrations: Kierra Jackson Designer
Cover Designer: Lerico Britton

ISBN-13: 978-1-951941-16-1

Printed in the United States of America

DEDICATION:
THIS SELF-HELP
GUIDE IS
DEDICATED TO
GOD'S PEOPLE ALL
OVER THE WORLD.
TO THE WOMEN
AND MEN OF EVERY
CULTURE, THIS ONE
IS FOR YOU!

ACKNOWLEDGMENT:
I WOULD LIKE TO
GIVE HONOR AND
PRAISE TO THE ONE
AND ONLY JESUS
CHRIST. YOUR
GUIDANCE
THROUGHOUT THIS
PROCESS WAS
EVERYTHING I
NEEDED AND MORE. I
COULD NOT HAVE
COMPLETED THIS
TASK WITHOUT YOU
AND FOR THAT I WILL
FOREVER BE
GRATEFUL!
I LOVE YOU, KIERRA

INTRODUCTION:
A BEAUTIFUL MESS IS A GUIDE DESIGNED TO ENCOURAGE, DEVELOP, AND ENHANCE WHO YOU ARE, WHO YOU'RE TRYING TO BECOME AND LEARNING THE DIFFERENCE BETWEEN THE TWO. THIS GUIDE HELPS YOU TO ANSWER DAILY QUESTIONS ABOUT YOU THAT YOU'VE ALWAYS WANTED TO KNOW GRACEFULLY AND UNAPOLOGETICALLY.

A *Beautiful* MESS

THE SAME GOD WHO INVITES YOU TO HIS THRONE OF GRACE IS THE SAME GOD WHO WILL GIVE YOU THE WORDS TO SAY WHEN YOU CAN'T FIND ANY WORDS OF YOUR OWN.

AM I STRUGGLING WITH THINGS I NEED TO RELEASE?

WHAT NEEDS DO I HAVE THAT AREN'T GETTING MET?

HOW CAN I BE MORE ENGAGED IN LIFE?

WHAT NEGATIVE THOUGHT PATTERNS DO I HAVE CONSISTENTLY?

What Makes Me Unique?

What Makes Me Unique?

Prayer Request

Beautiful Prayer

Lord, give me a heart like you. help me to see myself as you see me. Help me to be a better me. Shape me and make me confident as your child. May it all manifest in mercy, kindness and love. Lord my life shall bring you glory and by your grace, I shall win souls for your kingdom.
Amen

YOU ARE BUILT FOR THIS

BE STRONG IN THE LORD AND IN THE STRENGTH OF HIS MIGHT.
EPHESIANS 6:10

Beautiful Self-Worth Questions

How do I feel today?

Am I a happy person?

What makes me happy?

Do I enjoy my own company?

What made me smile today?

Scriptures on love:

Love Is:

My thoughts on what love should be:

ALTAR TIME
"LET US THEREFORE COME BOLDLY TO THE THRONE OF GRACE TO FIND HELP IN TIME OF NEED"
HEBREWS 4:16

TODAY, PLEASE HELP ME TO:

LORD, I ASK FORGIVNESS FOR:

TODAY, I SPEAK OVER:

Dear God,

WHAT VULNERABILITIES AM I AFRAID TO SHARE WITH OTHERS WHO LOVE ME?

_____

_____

_____

_____

_____

_____

_____

_____

_____

_____

WHAT AM I PASSIONATE ABOUT?

DOES MY LIVING SPACE REFLECT MY INNER WORLD?

HOW CAN I SPEND MORE TIME ON MY PASSION?

What Makes Me Unique?

What Makes Me Unique?

Prayer Request

Beautiful Prayer

Lord, help me to see the good in others, as well as myself.
Amen

YOU ARE LOVED

THIS IS MY COMMANDMENT THAT YOU LOVE OTHERS AS I HAVE LOVED YOU.
JOHN 15:12

Beautiful Self-Worth Questions

Am I on the right path?

Did I discover something new about myself today?

Do the people I surround myself with add any value to my life?

Am I following the crowd or am I listening to my own heart?

Do I take things personally?

Faithfulness

What is being faithful?

How can i apply it to my life?

Scriptures about faithfulness:

ALTAR TIME
"LET US THEREFORE COME BOLDLY TO THE THRONE OF GRACE TO FIND HELP IN TIME OF NEED"
HEBREWS 4:16

TODAY, PLEASE HELP ME TO:

LORD, I ASK FORGIVNESS FOR:

TODAY, I SPEAK OVER:

Dear God,

AM I ALLOWING FEAR TO HOLD ME BACK FROM GROWING?

WHAT ARE MY STRENGTHS?

AM I ALLOWING OTHERS TO DISTRACT ME?

WHAT IS MY VISION FOR THE NEXT FIVE YEARS?

What Makes Me Unique?

What Makes Me Unique?

Prayer Request

Beautiful Prayer

Lord, fill me with YOUR wisdom to help me resist any temptation that is attempting to make me fall, hurt or turn from you.

Teach me to guard my heart and cover me with your love.

Amen

 *YOU ARE NEVER ALONE*

*GOD IS WITH YOU
WHEREVER YOU MAY GO
AND NO MATTER WHAT LIFE
BRINGS.
1 JOHN 5:4*

Beautiful Self-Worth Questions

Did I step outside of my comfort zone today?

When was the last time I did something nice for myself?

Am I making too many excuses?

What do I want to be remembered for?

What do I need to let go of today?

Patience

Do i have patience/my thoughts?

What is patience?

Scriptures on patience:

ALTAR TIME
"Let us therefore come boldly to the throne of grace to find help in time of need"
Hebrews 4:16

TODAY, PLEASE HELP ME TO:

LORD, I ASK FORGIVNESS FOR:

TODAY, I SPEAK OVER:

Dear God,

DO I SEEK SOCIAL APPROVAL?

WHAT IS MY DEEPEST FEAR?

AM I HOLDING BACK LOVE FOR MYSELF?

AM I AFRAID TO SHOW OR EXPRESS LOVE?

What Makes Me Unique?

What Makes Me Unique?

Prayer Request

Beautiful Prayer

Lord, I thank you for my abilities, family, friends, health, love and most of all my life.
I will do amazing things in YOUR name.
Amen

YOU ARE AUTHENTIC

BLESSED ARE THE PURE IN HEART, FOR THEY WILL SEE GOD.
MATTHEW 5:8

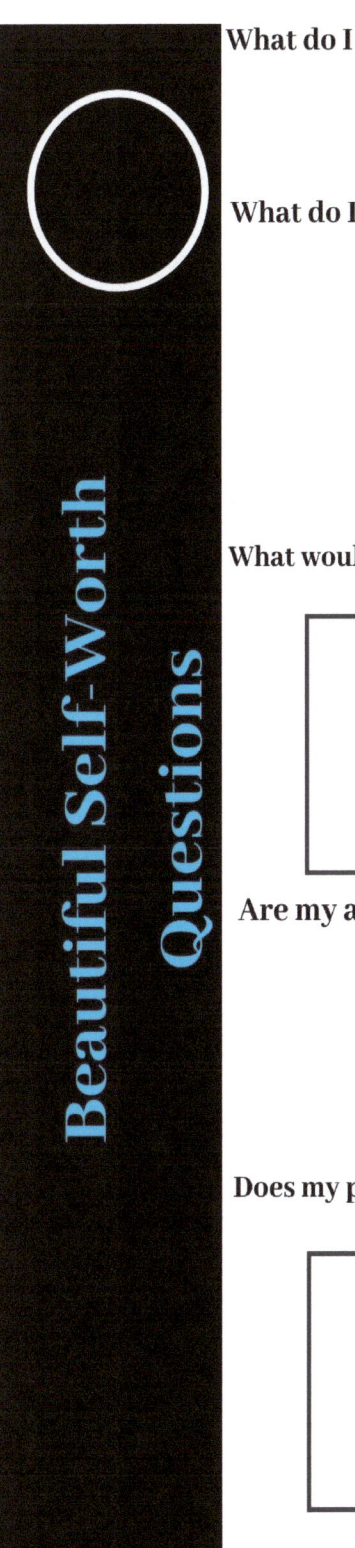

Beautiful Self-Worth Questions

What do I truly value?

What do I need to accept today that I can't change?

What would I do differently if I knew nobody would judge me?

Are my actions guided by fear or love?

Does my presence add value to those around me?

Strength

My thoughts about strength:

What is strength?

Scriptures about strength:

ALTAR TIME
"LET US THEREFORE COME BOLDLY TO THE THRONE OF GRACE TO FIND HELP IN TIME OF NEED"
HEBREWS 4:16

TODAY, PLEASE HELP ME TO:

LORD, I ASK FORGIVNESS FOR:

TODAY, I SPEAK OVER:

Dear God,

WHAT DOES LOVE MEAN TO ME?

AM I SPENDING ENOUGH TIME ON MY PRIORITIES?

_____

_____

_____

_____

_____

_____

_____

_____

_____

_____

WHO AM I?

HOW HAS MY CHILDHOOD AFFECTED MY LIFE?

What Makes Me Unique?

What Makes Me Unique?

Prayer Request

Beautiful Prayer

Lord, order my steps , and help me to stand firm when the winds of life are blowing strong. Amen

YOU ARE ENOUGH

YOU ARE A CHOSEN PERSON, A ROYAL PRIESTHOOD, A HOLY NATION, GOD'S SPECIAL POSSESSION, THAT YOU MAY DECLARE THE PRAISES OF HIM WHO CALLED YOU OUT OF DARKNESS INTO HIS WONDERFUL LIGHT.

1 PETER 2:9

Beautiful Self-Worth Questions

What do I think about when I'm alone?

What will give me joy today?

What can I do today that will be a unique expression of me?

What can I do to improve the quality of my life?

What's stopping me from enjoying my life?

My thoughts about peace:

What is peace?

Scriptures about peace

ALTAR TIME
"LET US THEREFORE COME BOLDLY TO THE THRONE OF GRACE TO FIND HELP IN TIME OF NEED"
HEBREWS 4:16

TODAY, PLEASE HELP ME TO:

LORD, I ASK FORGIVNESS FOR:

TODAY, I SPEAK OVER:

Dear God,

What Makes Me Unique?

Prayer Request

Beautiful Prayer

Lord, help me stay focused.

Amen

YOU ARE COURAGEOUS

HAVE I NOT COMMANDED YOU? BE STRONG AND COURAGEOUS. DO NOT BE FRIGHTENED, AND DO NOT BE DISMAYED, FOR THE LORD YOUR GOD IS WITH YOU WHEREVER YOU GO.
JOSHUA 1:9

What Makes Me Unique?

ALTAR TIME
"LET US THEREFORE COME BOLDLY TO THE THRONE OF GRACE TO FIND HELP IN TIME OF NEED"
HEBREWS 4:16

TODAY, PLEASE HELP ME TO:

LORD, I ASK FORGIVNESS FOR:

TODAY, I SPEAK OVER:

Beautiful Prayer

Lord, keep me walking in the safety of YOUR word.

Amen

YOU ARE VALUABLE

DO NOT FEAR FOR I HAVE REDEEMEND YOU. I HAVE CALLED YOU BY NAME, YOU ARE MINE. WHEN YOU PASS THROUGH THE WATER'S I WILL BE WITH YOU ; AND THROUGH THE RIVERS, THEY SHALL NOT OVERWHELM YOU. WHEN YOU WALK THROUGH FIRE YOU SHALL NOT BE BURNED, AND THE FLAME SHALL NOT CONSUME YOU. FOR I AM THE LORD YOUR GOD, YOUR SAVIOR.

ISAIAH 43:1-3

Dear God,

Dear God,

Dear God,

Kierra Jackson is a Certified Nursing Assistant who has worked in the medical field for over thirteen years. She is the CEO/Founder of Unapologetically Me which is a movement that empowers millennials to be Authentic and Courageous to live out their purpose on purpose. She has a beautiful daughter named Jaliyah and resides in Columbus, Georgia.